To: Wendy
  who knows

Women Also
Serve

Sylvia V. Whitlock
2017

D1417259

Women Also *Serve*

Duarte Invites *Women* to Join Rotary

S Y L V I A   W H I T L O C K

WOMEN ALSO SERVE
DUARTE INVITES WOMEN TO JOIN ROTARY

iUniverse books may be ordered through booksellers or by contacting:

iUniverse
1663 Liberty Drive
Bloomington, IN 47403
www.iuniverse.com
1-800-Authors (1-800-288-4677)

Because of the dynamic nature of the Internet, any web addresses or links contained in this book may have changed since publication and may no longer be valid. The views expressed in this work are solely those of the author and do not necessarily reflect the views of the publisher, and the publisher hereby disclaims any responsibility for them.

Any people depicted in stock imagery provided by Thinkstock are models, and such images are being used for illustrative purposes only. Certain stock imagery © Thinkstock.

ISBN: 978-1-4917-6059-8 (sc)
ISBN: 978-1-4917-6058-1 (e)

Library of Congress Control Number: 2015903307

Print information available on the last page.

iUniverse rev. date: 03/04/2015

This book is dedicated to the late Dr. Richard Key, who had the brilliant and brave idea to invite women into Rotary. As a superintendent of schools in the Duarte Unified School District, he had daily interaction with capable women, and as a proponent of Rotary service, he made a yet-undefined connection between the two.

This book is also dedicated to a past district governor, the late Dr. Tim Siu, who installed me as the first female Rotary club president "in the world." He was the first person I recall using that phrase, and he never passed up the opportunity to mention that fact whenever he and I were in the same vicinity. He was a believer in women in Rotary and was proud of his role in making it real.

Finally, I would be remiss if I did not salute the first woman who, in 1976, walked into a meeting of male Rotarians, Mary Lou Elliott. She escorted me to my first meeting some years later. Included in this dedication are all of the other women who have been firsts of one sort or another and have changed the face of Rotary.

Contents

Women Also Serve—
The Duarte Story

THIS BOOK IS ABOUT THE JOURNEY OF THE DUARTE ROTARY CLUB IN its quest to allow women to become members of Rotary. While the club's focus was not a bid for women's rights but for an increase in membership, the events played out as a women's-rights issue and attracted the attention of civil-rights proponents. I wrote this book in response to the many requests I received to tell the story.

In the Beginning

THE ROTARY CLUB OF DUARTE, CALIFORNIA, WAS CHARTERED IN District 530 in 1952. But alas, just before its twenty-fifth birthday, in 1976, it did an unacceptable thing in the eyes of Rotary International: the Duarte club violated Rotary's bylaws by inviting women to join in service above self, and its charter was unceremoniously revoked. Interestingly, when the first Rotary constitution, developed by the first Rotary Club of Chicago, was adopted in January 1906, it made no reference to the gender of potential Rotarians and specified only that they be persons of good character. No one knows why that statement morphed into "men of good character," but one might surmise that the change came because more men than women peopled the workforce at the time. In 1976, the Duarte battles were taking place in the shadow of the civil-rights era, when battles for civil rights, including women's rights, were rampant. Actually, the only issue the Duarte club was addressing was that membership was low, and there were lots of managerial-type women in Duarte who could make good Rotarians. "But," said an attorney from Rotary International, "they are forcing us to take everyone in, just like a motel."

At the time, Duarte was a small bedroom community, home to the renowned City of Hope Hospital. The ranking business, by size, was the Duarte Unified School District, presided over by Richard Key, superintendent of schools. Dr. Key was also the president of the soon-to-be-infamous Rotary Club of Duarte. In 1976, Superintendent Key looked around the school district for professional types who could make good Rotarians, but they were all women. (This was also a time when most of the persons invited to join Rotary were professionals, managers, business owners, and executives. It is still that way in many countries.) Dr. Key thought he would test the notion of inviting women. So he called the district governor elect, Paul Bryan; told him what he was contemplating; and asked for his opinion. The governor elect wryly suggested that perhaps allowing women into the club was a good idea, but as discretion was the better part of valor, he recommended that Dr. Key send in only first-name initials when he registered the new members with Rotary International. Obviously, the Four-Way Test had not yet been deeply rooted into the ethics of enterprising Rotarians.

Mary Lou Elliott, Donna Bogart, and Rosemary Freitag were invited to join the small club. Mary Lou was a junior-high-school principal, Donna was an elementary-school principal (later succeeded by Sylvia Whitlock), and Rosemary was a school psychologist. The women joined the group of eight or so male Rotarians, which included a real-estate agent, a dentist, an undertaker, a high-school principal, a City of Hope administrator, a Duarte City Council member, a sheriff, and the school superintendent. The undertaker resigned to register opposition to the invitation to the women. However, with the other male members, the women entered into the business of service above self and busied themselves with serving the community of which the school district was a large part. They were becoming Rotarians who entered into the spirit of this service organization. In 1977, they prepared to observe the twenty-fifth anniversary of the club and notified the head office of Rotary International of the celebration. RI, as it traditionally does, sent a representative to bear its greetings. All was well until the members of the club were introduced to the audience. The reaction of the representative went from surprise to disbelief to questioning to disbelief again and then to consternation as the women were introduced as Rotarians. In his experience and knowledge, there were no female Rotarians. The bylaws did not accommodate that. He returned to Evanston and reported on this disturbing series of events occurring in Duarte. Evanston immediately communicated with Duarte and told them the following:

- The bylaws did not permit female Rotarians.
- The Duarte club needed to ask the women to leave.
- If the women did not leave, the Duarte club had to cease calling itself a Rotary club.

The club took a vote of its members—minus the undertaker, who had already resigned from the club because he didn't like the fact that women had been invited—and decided it would not ask the women to leave. Instead, the members thought they would pursue some channels in the organization to change the bylaws. They asked to appeal to the board of directors but were told that only "real" Rotary clubs could have a hearing with the board of directors and that if the women continued to be present in their club, they were not a "real" Rotary club. The club pondered its options and realized that it could appeal to the Council on Legislation, the law-making body of Rotary International. The council was scheduled to meet in Tokyo that year.

The small Rotary club was already a force in the community, where all of its members were well known and visible.

Appealing to the Council on Legislation meant that someone had to attend the meeting, and the item had to be on the council's agenda. To finance the trip to Tokyo, the club had to raise a considerable amount of money. The community held bake sales and other fund-raising events to assist Duarte in sending a representative. Luke McJimpson, known affectionately as Mr. Rotary, a middle-school principal and a longtime member of the club, was chosen to speak to the case. Luke, with a great deal of hope, traveled to Tokyo to present Duarte's case. However, the manner in which the council articulated the case assured the defeat of the notion that women be allowed in Rotary. The issue presented was not whether women should be admitted to Rotary but whether the Duarte club had violated Rotary's bylaws by inviting women. The vote was 1,060 to 34, affirming the fact that the club had violated Rotary's bylaws.

Clearly, the thirty-four who voted against a violation by Duarte were trying to make a statement in support of allowing women to be admitted as members. When the international convention was held in Calgary, I met one of those thirty-four. I was riding a train from the suburbs to the convention center, and sitting across from me was a Rotarian and his wife. The gentleman looked at my badge, recognized the name Duarte, and asked if I had been a member of the infamous Ex-Rotary Club of Duarte. I gave him my largest smile of assent, and he proceeded to tell me that he had been a delegate to the Council on Legislation in Tokyo. He said, "I voted to have women in Rotary, because I have always thought they should be there."

His wife, a mature woman quietly sitting next to him, interrupted and said, "I didn't think so then, and I don't think so now!" Somewhat surprised at her response, I asked why. She responded, "Because our husbands are going out to meetings at night, and Lord knows who might be there."

I didn't bristle; I found the response ludicrous and told her that Rotary was a service club, not a social club, and that humanitarian projects were our objectives. Her opinion was not swayed and actually resembled the opinions of many women who were more vociferous than men were in their objections to women as members of Rotary clubs.

Interestingly, this was not the first time an issue about women had been brought before the Council on Legislation. When the council met in Detroit in 1950, a Rotary club from India suggested that the bylaws be changed to allow women members. The proposal was rejected, and the proponents went away. In Northern Ireland in 1912, the board of directors of the Belfast club discussed the advisability of electing women to Rotary membership or allowing them to attend Rotary meetings. The board of directors did not consider a female presence in Rotary to be desirable. Also, in 1912, Ida Buell of the Duluth, Minnesota, club spoke to the international convention, seeking to garner support for women's clubs. The convention did not support the idea. Starting in 1916, international boards approved women's auxiliaries, but by 1918, they reversed that decision and refused to recognize women as any part of official Rotary. I will discuss the Seattle 15 group, which faced a similar issue, later.

Luke returned to Duarte empty-handed. What would the club do? They had already decided they liked having the female members and would not ask them to leave. It wasn't long before RI sent a representative to Duarte, on March 27, 1978, to remove the charter of the club. It was the ultimate blow, but the Rotary Club of Duarte did not go away quietly. It simply put an X over the Rotary symbol and renamed itself the Ex-Rotary Club of Duarte. There is actually an Ex-Rotary Club of Duarte pin. The group continued to serve the community as it had before the women were invited. Into this club, I, a new principal in the Duarte Unified School District, was invited. It did not occur to me that I could refuse the invitation, because as a new elementary-school principal, I was interested in serving the community.

As a child, growing up with my grandparents in Jamaica, I watched my grandmother illustrate service above self daily. She set the pattern for what my life would become. We were not rich or privileged, but we had enough to share, and that was what she taught me to do. I used to carefully save money from my small allowance to put into the offering plate on Sunday, and I ran errands for neighbors who needed my help—sometimes to complete an errand my grandmother had started. That was how I was taught life should be—people should help each other. When I returned to New York City and went to work for the United Nations after college, the experience put another layer on my notion of service. I did what seemed right. I contributed, via payroll deductions, to United Way. I donated blood at the Red Cross regularly. But there was never a face on the beneficiaries of anything I was doing in those places. I went through the motions. The Rotary Club of Duarte gave me my first experience in putting faces and needs together. I joined my colleagues in identifying and meeting the needs of the community in which we worked. We did not engage in international projects, because without the facilitation offered by Rotary International, to which we no longer had access, it was difficult. We were busy with holding barbecues; providing Easter, Thanksgiving, and Christmas baskets; reading to students; helping to sponsor field trips for students; and generally serving the needy.

We were not content, however, to be outcasts of one of the greatest humanitarian organizations in the world. An attorney from a neighboring Rotary club, Sanford Smith from the Rotary Club of Arcadia, a club that had sponsored us, suggested we try enlisting the help of the American Civil Liberties Union and taking the case through the courts. We took his advice, which he offered pro bono, and gave notice to Rotary International that we would file suit to be reinstated. The suit was scheduled to be filed in a California superior court. Rotary International petitioned that a federal court should hear the case, because as it said, not all members of the board of directors were Californians. There was, however, a more probable reason for that petition: in a New York case, the federal court had ruled that a private club could exercise exclusionary rights over its membership, and that favorable ruling would have been a precedent for Rotary International. The federal court ruled that the case be heard in California.

The case was filed in June 1978 in a California superior court. It was pressed by American Civil Liberties Union attorney Fred Okrand. The club claimed that the exclusion of women violated the state's Unruh Act, which prohibited discrimination by any business establishment.

Judge Max Deutz, presiding, ruled that Rotary International was not a business establishment, so the act did not apply. He refused to reinstate the club. The Duarte club, defended by Sanford Smith, an attorney and Rotarian from Arcadia, also claimed that association with other members promoted one in his or her own business or profession, so women should have a constitutional right to that association. However, Deutz wrote a ten-page opinion, saying in part, "The women applicants were already engaged in a business or profession and no employment was denied them. They were merely denied the privilege of joining with individuals from other vocations, professions and businesses in a community service." Strike one! From that experience, we learned that despite the climate of the times, when equal rights were a hotly debated issue, this pursuit was not going to be a pushover.

We added several other women to our Rotary club. They included Donna Georgino, who was assistant director of the Parks and Recreation Department in Duarte; Elaine Benthuys, administrator from the City of Hope Medical Center; and Marabelle Taylor, a much-traveled resident of Westminster Gardens. Women and men served together without incident. In 1985, I was selected to be the 1987–88 president of Duarte Rotary Club, and Donna Georgino was selected to be the president elect.

The club members and attorneys, including Sanford Smith, regrouped and appealed the decision to an appellate court in California. This time, the defense again used California's Unruh Act, which prohibited discrimination in public accommodations. Because of the classification system used in the recruitment of members, the networking effect, and the fact that, at that time, about 80 percent of members had their dues paid by their employers, Rotary was deemed a public accommodation. In a forty-nine-page decision written by Eugene McClosky, who was a justice of the Second District Court of Appeal, the superior-court decision was overturned, and it was ruled that women should not be denied admission to Rotary. In his decision, McClosky wrote, "Incredibly, 14 years before the start of the 21ˢᵗ Century and 210 years after the signing of the Declaration of Independence, we still find ourselves having to write an opinion defending the right of American women to equal opportunity in a secular organization of approximately 20,000 clubs with more than 900,000 members." McClosky went on to refer to Rotary's Four-Way Test, which reads as follows:

Is it the truth?
Is it fair to all concerned?
Will it build goodwill and better friendships?
Is it beneficial to all concerned?

Justice McClosky wrote, "While the Rotary organizations are in large part very well-motivated and accomplish much good, International's discriminatory policy toward women clearly violates this test and evidences International's failure to practice toward women the fairness 'to all' that it preaches." The appellate justices also said it was unnecessary to decide the case on the Duarte club's additional argument that the men-only rule violated women's state constitutional right to pursue a business or profession. They disagreed strongly with Deutz's opinion that excluding women did not interfere with that constitutional right, noting, as previously mentioned, that most employers paid Rotary members' dues because they considered membership good for business. McClosky wrote,

> This evidence leaves no doubt that business concerns are a motivating factor in joining local clubs. While Rotarians perform numerous and considerable charitable services at the local, national and international levels, the evidence establishes that there are business benefits enjoyed and capitalized upon by Rotarians and their businesses or employers and it has, in effect, provided a forum which encourages business relations to grow and which enhances the commercial advantages of its members.

This decision was now incumbent on all California clubs. However, Rotary did not accept this ruling quietly. An attorney for Rotary International, William John Kennedy, announced he would appeal to the California Supreme Court and, if necessary, to the United States Supreme Court. In the meantime, the Duarte club did not have to be reinstated. Carol Agate, representing the American Civil Liberties Union, and Kennedy agreed that the impact of the appellate court ruling was wide and, if not reversed, could force all organizations to open membership to interested persons. Deutz had ruled on the rights of a service club, as a private club, to restrict its membership, but the appellate justices saw Rotary as a business establishment providing goods and services to its members. The case was appealed to the California Supreme Court, which refused to hear the case, essentially affirming the appellate court's decision.

There were rumblings about inviting women to join Rotary in other districts and other clubs. In 1984, District 5030, in Washington State, was about to start a new Rotary club. District Governor Carl Swenson appointed a Rotarian to start the Rotary Club of Seattle International Districts. The club filed its charter application but deleted all references to specific genders. RI rejected its application. It was resubmitted with the appropriate "male" and "men" references and duly chartered on September 18, 1984. In 1986, the new Seattle club took a resolution for the admission of women to the Council on Legislation. The resolution was defeated. However, in defiance, the club admitted fifteen women in 1986 and registered them with Rotary International. General Secretary Phillip Lindsey advised the club that it was in violation of the rules and would have its charter terminated if it remained so. In January 1987, the Seattle club filed an amicus brief with the United States Supreme Court, in support of our Duarte club. In 1987, Oakland 3 Rotary Club also went on record as opposing the dechartering of the Duarte club.

So now the appellate court had ruled that women had to be admitted to Rotary, with a decision incumbent only on California clubs. The year was 1986, and I was the president elect for the Rotary Club of Duarte. I was duly invited to President Elect Training Seminar (PETS), scheduled to be held at the Doubletree Hotel in Orange County on March 13–15, 1987.

The postcard invitation I received reminded me, "Bring your coat and tie, because directory pictures will be taken." PETS was hosted by Districts 526, 528, 530, 532, 533, and 534. (Each district later added a zero to its district number.) I guess old habits die hard, and they felt it was unnecessary to change the PETS invitation stock for a single female president elect. With some trepidation—I didn't know what to expect—I made my reservation and packed a wardrobe of conservative business attire.

I arrived early at the hotel and registered without incident. I went to my room and dressed for dinner. My seat at dinner was assigned, which saved me the awkwardness of having to look around for an acceptable seat. I knew no one at the seminar. I sat at a table with nine men who were the epitome of politeness and courtesy. Some were interested and supportive. Some did not speak directly to me. Many came over from other tables and asked questions about my club. There were 310 male attendees and me, the only woman. I was introduced to Pablo Campos Lynch, a past district governor and director from Mexico City, then District 417. He was warm and gracious and told me to make notes about the weekend because, he said, "It is a historic occasion. You are the first female president elect to attend a Rotary training session as a president elect." I was asked to have my picture taken with Pablo and Dr. Tim Siu, District 530's governor elect. Sadly, I did not ask to have any of those pictures.

The following morning, after breakfast, I attended my first information session, which focused on Rotary International. The decision of the California appellate court, which had sanctioned my presence at this event, was discussed, and it was reported that it was Rotary International's intention to appeal the decision to the United States Supreme Court, because as the sitting governor John Fee so indelicately characterized it, "it is just a case of the mouse that roared—a small club trying to change Rotary International." I sat in that gathering more than incensed at John's characterization of our club. I also found it difficult to believe that the esteemed Supreme Court of the United States of America would deign to take on the issue of women in a service club. We were not *Roe v. Wade* or *Brown v. the Board of Education of Topeka, Kansas*. I had not grabbed on to the notion that this was a human-rights issue—women's rights—which had just as important a value as anything with which the court had dealt. I thought John was misstating Rotary's intent. (Over the years, since that incident, John and I have grown a healthy respect for each other. He and his wife, June, are some of my favorite people in Rotary.) I left, determined to put the "mouse that roared" in Rotary's history books. The first thing my club did upon my return was design a new banner: Rotary Club of Duarte—The Mouse That Roared. The banner included the phrase "Equal Opportunity for Service." The rest of the seminar went downhill. Sans coat and tie, I had my directory picture taken. The best thing about the configuration of men and woman that weekend was that during restroom breaks, there were long lines outside the men's restrooms, and I could sashay past them into the empty ladies' room.

Most of the weekend was a blur of pictures, questions, smiles, handshakes, and notes. I left on Sunday morning, trained, as mandated for president elects, to take on the role of president of the Rotary Club of Duarte.

I assiduously studied the *President's Manual* and set about putting together my team. Of considerable help was Mary Lou Elliott, who was the first woman invited to the Duarte Rotary Club, a fellow principal, and my adviser. DGE (District Governor Elect) Dr. Siu asked me to serve on the district's finance committee. DG (District Governor) Taro Kawa later invited me to chair the district's Four-Way Test Speech Contest. I remember asking him to give me the records of the previous years so that I could determine the procedures, and his response was that there were no records. Therefore, I reinvented the Four-Way Test Speech Competition and established some procedures that are still being used. I continued to chair that competition for six years and left it with clear guidelines for my successors. That position allowed me to meet many of my fellow Rotarians, especially the Rotarians in Nevada. Concurrently, I chaired the Ambassadorial Scholarship Committee, of which I had been a member for two years. Those two assignments served me well when, as district governor, I was looking for Rotarians to serve with me on my leadership team.

Rotary International did appeal the case to the United States Supreme Court. A scant four months after the case went to the Supreme Court, on May 4, 1987, I was on my way to school, when the news on the radio announced that the Supreme Court of the United States had ruled that service clubs could not exclude women. Driving west on the 210 freeway, I looked around me to see if I could discern anyone else listening to the announcement. I knew it was a big piece of news. Although it had taken eleven years to get to this place, the Supreme Court's action had come earlier than we'd expected. In the twenty or so minutes it took me to drive to school, I wondered how our small club would handle this decision. The news had been announced on the East Coast, which was three hours ahead of California's Pacific time, so West Coast media had a lot of time to prepare before we all awakened to the news.

I arrived at my campus to a bevy of reporters and television cameras and, with some difficulty, made my way from my car to my office. I was unprepared for this! Students clustered and clowned around the cameras. There was general pandemonium. With flashbulbs going off in my face, I was asked if I would submit to an interview. First, I had to explain to the students that something good had happened and that they needed to go to their classrooms. Mercifully, the superintendent called and said I needed to leave the campus and come to the district office. I made sure my absence would be covered. I got in my car and, trailed by the reporters, left for the three-minute drive to the district office. There, Mary Lou and Dr. Key were in the boardroom with a veteran newscaster, Warren Olney. I have had a lot of years to figure out how all this transpired so quickly that morning. The news was first announced on the East Coast, three hours ahead of those of us in California, so by the time the West Coast awakened to the news, the media had had three hours to get ready and dispatch their reporters. The surprise to us was that it was such big news. I have also had a lot of time to think about why that event was important. What had started as just a membership-development action for us had had a farther-reaching impact in the world of civil rights. We were advocating for the Rotary Club of Duarte's survival. The world saw the human-rights issue. The result of the Supreme Court ruling extended far beyond Duarte and beyond Rotary International.

Mary Lou Elliott, Dr. Key, Warren Olney, a photographer, and I sat around a large table in the boardroom. Warren asked many questions about the timeline of the event and about Rotary International, including its mission and purpose. He directed most of his questions at me, the incoming president of the Duarte club, trained by Rotary International and ready to assume office as the first female president in Rotary International. To all of his questions, I thought I gave studied and intelligent answers. After about four hours of questioning, as the interview trailed off and seemed to be drawing to a close, I started to prepare to leave. As I got to my feet, he said, "Tell me, Sylvia—how did you get chosen to be president of the Duarte club?"

In a moment of sheer carelessness, I answered (like a true Rotarian), "Oh, I don't know. I must have missed a meeting." I had no clue how much I would bemoan that answer, although the lessons it taught me were many. That evening, the Supreme Court decision was the top of the news. In spite of the hours of material Warren Olney gathered that I considered good copy, the segment that aired was my careless final answer. I have had a long time to think about what naysayers to women in Rotary must have thought about that answer. But I learned a few things that day, especially about staying in character if there's a camera in your face. Through all subsequent interviews, I maintained my conservative Rotary-woman demeanor. The news was widely publicized. I counted eleven front-page articles, including the *New York Times*, the *Los Angeles Times*, the *Herald Tribune*, and many other local and national newspapers. I do not know how the topic was covered overseas.

We received many telephone calls, none of which was insulting, although we did receive a call that asked if the food was any better in Rotary now that there were female members. I responded that the Rotary women were not preparing the food. Some calls were less pleasant and not about women in Rotary.

The afternoon of the day the Supreme Court decision was announced, Donna Georgino, Bill Brooks, Mary Lou, a few others, and I attended a reception hosted by one of the attorneys from the American Civil Liberties Union, Carol Agate. The ACLU had helped to carry the case through the courts. Sanford Smith was ecstatic. Dr. Key was a hero. It takes a Rotarian to invite someone to join Rotary, so without Dr. Key's invitation, none of these triumphs would have happened. I have received a lot of recognition, because that day, my title became "the first female president of a Rotary club in the world." The women in the club did not engage in any of the struggle in the courts. It was carried by attorneys who argued the principles involved in the issue. We continued to serve our community and represent Rotary with integrity and purpose.

The Aftermath of the
Supreme Court Ruling

THE DUARTE CLUB MET IN A LITTLE CAFÉ ON HUNTINGTON DRIVE—
the site where the charter had been removed from the club's possession.
Because the club was now a curiosity, we had to move the meeting to
a site that could accommodate more people—members and visitors—
so we relocated to the golf club on Huntington Drive. Each meeting
found members answering questions and entertaining numerous
visitors and members of the press. From England, Germany, and
France, Rotarians came to visit the Duarte club and see how and
what we were doing. Articles about our club showed up in German
and Korean Rotarian newsletters. Strangely silent was the *Rotarian*,
Rotary International's official newsletter. We did not receive a
"welcome back" from Rotary International, but they sent us a new
dues schedule. It was not until April 2004 that the *Rotarian* released
an issue with the profiles of three women on the cover and the byline
"Role Models—An In-Depth Look at How Women Bring Strength
and Vitality to Rotary Clubs." Deputy Editor Wayne Hearn's page
was headlined with a question: Why devote both this month's cover
and "In Focus" section to the topic of women in Rotary? He wrote,

> A somewhat flip answer is: Why not? After all, this
> Rotary year, (2004) marks the 15th anniversary of the
> landmark decision by the 36th Council on Legislation to

allow Rotary clubs to admit women. In January 1989, council members, meeting in Singapore voted 328 to 117—a 75 percent majority—in favor of the measure which was advanced by current RI President Jonathan Majiyagbe, another timely link to the present.

In 2004, about 12 percent of Rotarians were women.

Back to 1987. That was the beginning of the Polioplus campaign. We, the Duarte club, had to settle down and continue the business of Rotary, which included raising money for the Rotary Foundation. All of our members became Paul Harris Fellows and responded to the Polioplus requests. We were also invited to participate at the district level, and I mentioned that Governor Nominee Designate Taro Kawa had asked me to chair the Four-Way Test Speech Competition. I was a school principal with ready access to hundreds of students. I continued to chair that committee for several years and worked successfully with all the male Rotarians I encountered. The following year, I was asked to be a member of the district's budget and finance committee. I sensed no awkwardness whatsoever in my dealings with male members of other clubs.

Club Pursuits

THE SMALL ROTARY CLUB OF DUARTE WAS IMMERSED IN THE BUSINESS
of Rotary. Included in our membership, among others, was a member
of the sheriff's department, the school-district superintendent, a
director of recreation for the city, a city councilman, an administrator
at the City of Hope Hospital, a junior-high-school principal, a
journalist, a psychologist, and a dentist. I mention these because in
our efforts to serve the community, they had invaluable knowledge
and contacts.

In 1987, our first international adventure as a reinstated club
was to adopt an orphanage in Mexico, in Baja California, about a
three-hour drive from Duarte. We held a yard sale to raise money for
the orphanage. Our recreation director arranged games and sports
activities for the children on the day of our visit. Our dentist, along
with other dental volunteers, worked on giving examinations and
attending to identified needs. We took toothbrushes, toothpaste,
dental floss, and vitamins. We collected clothes, books, toys, and
food and took them down every six weeks. Our partner in this
endeavor was a Rotary club in Ensenada. We continued to support
that orphanage until it closed.

Each Christmas, we organized an event called Pancake Breakfast
with Santa Claus. Our Rotarian with a long white beard, Dale
Spickler, was our Santa Claus for about six years. Members made
and served pancakes on the morning of the event. Local vendors and

restaurants supplied the ingredients for the breakfast and toys for the community's children. All we had to provide was the elbow grease. Members bought the tickets and distributed them at local schools.

We used Rotary matching grants to establish an HIV/AIDS center in Port Antonio, Jamaica, and with the help of a Discovery Grant, we sent a team from our club—a physician, a technology expert, and a social worker—to help the group organize their outreach to the community. We also sent a team to Nigeria, where, with the help of a matching grant, we sank water wells in a small community from which women had had to walk many miles to fetch water.

In 1989, after an impassioned speech by Frank Devlyn, who was international president elect, the Council on Legislation voted to eliminate the requirement in the RI constitution that membership in Rotary clubs be limited to men. Rotary clubs around the world welcomed women.

While the face of Rotary around the world has changed, there is much room for growth. The percentage of women in Rotary in the United States of America is about 34 percent, while the world percentage hovers around 18 percent. Women are, however, moving through the ranks of officers. In 1995, Mimi Altmann of the Deerfield, Illinois, club became the first female district governor, in District 6440, followed closely by Gilda Chirafisi in District 7230, Janet Holland in District 5790, Riba Lovrein in District 5220, Virginia Nordby in District 6380, Donna Rapp in District 6310, Ann Robertson in District 6710, and Olive Scott in District 7190. As club presidents attend PETS, all district governors around the world are mandated to attend the International Assembly for training. With about 530 district governors from around the world in attendance, being part of this group, the large majority of whom were men, was probably a daunting experience for these United States district governors. It was 2001–02 before the first female district governor, Margaret Cooker, was appointed, in District 5300. Since then, in this district, there have been only three other female district governors: Christine Montan, Barbara Risher-Welch, and me.

I think we have undoubtedly demonstrated to Rotarians and all other interested observers that women are capable of serving with the best of men—in the trenches, around the board tables, in financial negotiations, and wherever our mystique is at work. Past RI president Majiyagbe remarked, "Women serve alongside men in almost every area of employment, as physicians, professors, engineers, construction workers and business executives. It is only reasonable that they should serve as Rotarians."

Is discrimination against women alive and well? You bet it is! Are women recognized for what they are contributing to Rotary causes? You bet they are! Why aren't they being tapped for responsible positions in Rotary International? Where is the disconnect? An editorial in the 1990 issue of the *Rotarian* characterized female Rotarians as accomplished, talented, and concerned about their families, communities, nations, and world. Perhaps when women receive more recognition in international offices, they will cease being referred to as "female Rotarians." Some of their appointments are listed below.

In 2005, Carolyn Jones of Alaska became the first woman appointed as trustee of the Rotary Foundation.

In 2008, Catherine Noyes-Riveau of France began her term as the first woman elected to the RI board of directors.

In 2012, the late Elizabeth Demaray began her term as international treasurer, the first woman to serve in that position.

In 2013, Anne Matthews began her term as the first woman to serve as RI vice president, to Oklahoma's Ron Burton. She was also the second female foundation trustee and the third woman elected to the RI board of directors.

Clearly, there is much room at the top, but women must negotiate the various steps to take through the levels in the organization before they may be placed in those ranks. A member must be a club president before he or she may be a zone director, and he or she must be a zone director before he or she may be placed on the international board.

My first attendance at an international convention was in 1987 in Philadelphia, where Donna Georgino and I were the only female Rotarians present. We blended into the populace, but a few Rotarians scrutinized our badges. Ultimately, they invited us into their conversations and celebrations. I remember thinking, when I attended my first district conference, that it was quite a change from the gatherings that had characterized our club meetings. We were learning about projects and needs in our district community that we had not even begun to imagine. At the first international convention, the kaleidoscopic image of attendees from different countries—the colorful native dress, the different languages, the flag presentations, the interest sessions—overwhelmingly reaffirmed our choice to be part of the organization known as Rotary International.

Rotary International Presidents

I HAVE MET EVERY PRESIDENT OF ROTARY INTERNATIONAL SINCE THE United States Supreme Court ruled on the Duarte case. They have been cordial and encouraging. The 2013–14 president, Ron Burton, gave me the opportunity to be on the world stage by asking me to address the 2013 International Assembly. In response to many requests from members and officers to do so, I have included that address and some of my other speeches here, but more importantly, I have included comments from some of the Rotary International presidents—the men who have led the almost 1.3 million members of Rotary and who made specific welcoming comments to me or about the issue of women in Rotary. They all responded to my request to contribute to this book. I have transcribed, verbatim, their submissions.

I have also included comments from some other women who were firsts in their positions in Rotary.

Mary Lou Elliott, the first woman invited by Dr. Key, recounts her memories for inclusion in this book thusly:

> As I remember it:
>
> I was a middle school principal in 1976 when Richard Key, the School Superintendent in Duarte, approached me about becoming a member of the local Rotary Club. I questioned him about the fact that Rotary was known

as an all-male club. He assured me that this would not be a problem. He was given permission to submit my name to Rotary International using first name initials and my last name. There were only about six members attending the first meeting I visited. It was explained that to be a real service to the community there needed to be more members and the majority of new leaders were women. Women were in leadership roles at the City of Hope—a prominent research hospital, in a local bank and in the school district.

After visiting the club meeting, I was once again assured that there would be no problem with my membership and there would be invitations going to other women. I was not involved in any other service club, other than helping my husband in his involvement in the Lions Club in Glendora where we lived. I thought it was a great idea to become involved in Duarte where I worked.

I had worked in Duarte for close to twenty years and knew the needs of the community. I never thought of membership in the Duarte Rotary Club as part of the women's movement. I was only concerned with what could be done to serve. The club, at the time that I agreed to join, had adopted an orphanage in Mexico and supported families that had children in City of Hope Hospital, especially during holidays. I was taken into the club in 1976 as M. L. Elliott and became a full member of the Duarte Rotary Club. Rotary International accepted my membership. Meetings were held weekly, practicing the values of Rotary. The club grew, adding both men and women.

To celebrate the club's twenty-fifth anniversary, a dinner was held. District Rotary and other dignitaries were invited. The dinner was enjoyed until Dr. Key asked the members of the club to stand. When the members, including three women, stood, there was an uneasy feeling. We didn't feel there had been any wrongdoing on our part as it seemed okay to include women that fit needed classifications to keep membership viable.

Dr. Key was told, during the week, to either get rid of the women members or relinquish the club charter.

At the following regular meeting, Dr. Key shared the ultimatum with the members present. The women offered to step down rather than cause the loss of the charter. A vote was taken and all but one member voted to keep the female membership. The one dissenting voter left the club. When the decision was sent to the Rotary District, action was taken and the charter was revoked.

Sanford Smith, a private attorney, offered to represent the club to sue Rotary California District and Rotary International for reinstatement. An ACLU representative assisted Smith.

Local and national television stations sent reporters to witness the actual handing over of the club charter and the cutting of the chain holding the Rotary Wheel in front of the Crystal Café where the club met.

The club continued to meet, deciding to keep the name, Duarte Rotary Club, by placing *ex* in front of the title. The membership pins for the ExRotary Club of Duarte had a large *X* placed over the Rotary symbol.

The philosophy of the club continued to be that of Rotary International excluding the problem area. The rest is history. Court cases were marked by rejection, then success, and finally, acceptance after more than ten years. Never once during that period could Rotary International have accused the ExRotary Club of Duarte of practicing anything but the true Rotary spirit.

I left the club in 1989 when I moved to Oregon. I attended a Rotary luncheon in Springfield, Oregon, when I was invited by one of their members. I was encouraged to submit membership papers to join the club. However, at the following meeting, I was told there was not a position for me in the club. In all fairness, I wasn't told that I was rejected because I was female, but I didn't see any attending women.

I am now an honorary member of the El Camino Rotary Club in Oceanside, California.

Comments from Past Rotary International Presidents

PRIP (2003–04) Jon Majiyagbe sent me the following note:

August 16, 2014 at 1:02 p.m.
Dear PDG Sylvia,

You requested me some weeks ago to write up about my feelings and involvement with Women In Rotary. I wanted to make sure I gave my best assistance on a topic that is very dear to my heart. On arriving home after attending to my health challenges abroad, I searched in vain for newspaper cuttings about the issue which I had wanted to send to you.

I do sincerely regret the delay and if you have not completed your work and will like some input, below is a brief write-up.

WOMEN IN ROTARY

In the wake of the decision of the U. S. Supreme Court about the gender provision of the Rotary International Constitution, there was a profusion of arguments as to why the organisation should break up; one part for the

Americans to respect their "own laws" and the other for the rest of the world.

Non-legal minds wondered why an international organisation should ignore the cultures of other nations as regards the participation of women. The underlying force beneath the veneer of various arguments is that most clubs cannot accept that women should join them in their meetings. Why couldn't women limit themselves to the International Inner Wheel Movement or, at best, form their own Rotary clubs. The more vociferous men decided it was time to quit Rotary.

The Board of Rotary International could not brook any argument since the organisation and its Foundation were incorporated in the United States. RI has the obligation to amend its constitution to remove the gender inequality in our provisions. The Board at that time was headed by the RI President from Australia, late Mr. Royce Abbey.

He took steps to make preparations for the next Council on Legislation by empanelling a committee of some members of the Board and staff of RI to review all proposed enactments and resolutions relevant to the topic for appropriate presentation by the Board thus ensuring favourable passage.

Apart from other issues considered was the selection of the Board delegate to present arguments for Rotary, the Rotary International Board. In the opinion of everyone, this was better handled by an attorney. With about four of the members of the Board defending the classification of Law, one Director Allen of the US was selected.

Allen could not travel to Singapore for some important reasons and the mantle fell on me as substitute to present the case for opening the door to female membership by amending the RI constitution.

In Singapore, a special date and time was allocated for this important item and quite a lot of heightened interest was generated by Rotarians and non-Rotarians alike. Some members of the public were allowed to witness the proceedings with emotions charged on all sides.

I proposed to the Council that there was need, indeed, an obligation to respect the judgement of the Supreme Court of the United States and so amend our constitution by removing the male gender provision. I argued that it was right to admit women who could be wives or daughters of Rotarians and other relatives and indeed the induction of new members could include other professional ladies, either single or married.

What did it matter, I posted, if ladies joined our ranks, the important criteria is that they are of impeccable character and have a vocation or profession. The days were long gone when women's activities were confined to the home. They are now working alongside men in every area of employment—engineers, doctors, attorneys—and occupy eminent positions in all human endeavors. Whatever men did, women could also do, and sometimes, better than men. Allowing women to join Rotary would only help increase our membership and provide more hands to render service to the community.

Opponents of the resolution were equally forceful and spoke eloquently and with great emotion. Although a time limit was imposed when so many people wanted to contribute to the debate, quite a few threw caution to the wind and exceeded the time allotted. One speaker said our intended decision would result in people leaving the organisation.

When called upon to respond, I closed my remarks by stating that although the subject was not exhausted, we were, and it was fitting for the human family to come together in meetings to make the world a better place.

Looking back today, I believe our steps were justified. Our meetings have, not only become more colourful, but are also enhanced by the important contributions made by women. Their impact on the organisation must have influenced me to introduce the concept of the "Family of Rotary."

Kind regards,
Jon Majiyagbe

I met Charles Keller, Rotary International president from 1987 to 1988, in 1987 at a Foundation event held on the Queen Mary in Long Beach. He was interested in my road to the presidency of the Duarte Club.

Bringing women into Rotary was a by-product of the expanding role women played in the business and professional world in the 20th century. I always understood why Rotary grew as a male organization beginning in 1905 … women were primarily involved in the home. The change was gradual. In my law school class in 1947, there were only 5 women of 105 members. Today, each law school class is about 50-50. Rotary first addressed the issue at the 1977 Council on Legislation in San Francisco. I was in the chair when an hour or more of vigorous debate occurred. It failed by a 2/3 to 1/3 vote, despite the fact that some of Rotary's strongest leaders supported the change. *But the issue was on the table and the Rotary world over the next years and at the Council on Legislation meetings in Chicago in 1980 and in Monte Carlo in 1983, both of which I chaired, got closer and closer to the change. By 1986 (when I was president elect) the COL gave almost 65 percent approval to the change ... but it took a 2/3 vote. I can recall Matt Capares and Cliff Dochterman and Walter Maddocks and other leaders making powerful arguments that it was time to make the change.* I had no doubt it would pass at the next COL meeting in 1989, and it did, with an assist on May 22, 1987 from the United States Supreme Court. It was interesting to me that Matt Capares as President, at his last Board meeting in 1987, took action to require all Rotary Clubs in countries where the law required it, to admit qualified women to Rotary Clubs. That was the real beginning and when I took over as President on July 1, 1987, I found that in addition to promoting the Polio Plus campaign, my largest single issue as I traveled the world, was to help Rotary Clubs in regions with different cultures, to adjust to the new reality. To their credit, most Rotarians were ready for the change, and adjusted to it. As you might expect, there were some surprises but over the last 25 years, Rotary Clubs, with few exceptions, have embraced the business and professional leaders who happened to be women. Not only have they been active, enthusiastic club members, but they are increasingly doing their share in our leadership ranks,-district governors, directors, trustees, and next year the vice president will be a woman. But I am always reminded that the real contribution has nothing to do with gender. They have simply become skilled participants in the business and professional world from which we draw our strength and members. In my club, the California, PA. Rotary Club, we are now about 50-50 and the women members as leaders and in everything we do (including my wife) take their turns. I suspect that women are by nature "givers" and that is what makes a real Rotarian. I have a hundred stories on this subject, but perhaps this chronology will be a help to you.

... Best Wishes ... Chuck Keller, PRIP 1987–88

The following are comments that PRIP Cliff Dochterman made in a speech given in 2012, forwarded to me for inclusion here. I consider Cliff a true friend whose prolific authoring skills have regaled me for a long time. Cliff is the author of As I Was Saying and other books about his experiences as a Rotarian. I was his aide at the 2013 Southern California and Nevada PETS, an assignment that was an honor.

Cliff Dochterman
President, Rotary International 1992–93
May 18, 2012
Rotary Club of Moraga

WOMEN IN ROTARY 25TH ANNIVERSARY

Now I know what it is like to be the token male at a very interesting Rotary event—Women in Rotary. However, I am proud to be on a program with these women who have contributed so much to Rotary International.

In 1981, under the leadership of President Stan McCaffrey, I chaired a significant international group of Rotarians, called the New Horizons Committee, to take a look at what might or should happen in the future of Rotary. Among our 30 recommendations, in addition to beginning a worldwide polio immunization program was the proposal that the membership of Rotary should be opened to women members.

As I look back over 30 years, I suspect that those two visions of Rotary's future—Polio Plus and women in Rotary—have been the most influential factors in my entire Rotary experience.

I clearly recall attending the Council on Legislation in Singapore in 1989 as a voting delegate. It was a personal pleasure to have a chance to speak on behalf of the enactment to eliminate the word *male* from the Constitutional documents of Rotary International. The issue was strongly opposed by some delegates.

My comments were along the line that Rotary "stands at a crossroad"—which way will we go? I recall speaking to that Legislative Session that "Rotary had certainly stood at a crossroad numerous times in its 80 year history. We were at a crossroad when Rotary moved to Canada in 1910, and someone must have said "You mean someone can be a Rotarian even if they don't live in the United States?"

Then, I'm sure there were those at the crossroad when Rotary moved into Cuba in 1915, and someone asked, "You mean you are going to have Rotarians who don't even speak English?"

And certainly Rotary was at a crossroad when Rotarians asked, "Can we admit persons of another race or ethnic group—who are Asians from China and Japan in 1920 or people from Africa?" Just as Rotary moved forward in those historic moments—the time had come to eliminate all gender restrictions. When we took the vote, the constitutional change was adopted. It was a great step for Rotary International. It was headline news around the world.

However, the introduction of women into Rotary was not universally embraced. When I was President of Rotary there were a few Clubs which advised me that their Club does not admit women members. So, I had to write to those Clubs and say that if their Club had by laws which actually refused to admit women, then it was a violation of the RI Constitution, and I had no alternative but to remove their Club's charter. If they just did not invite women then I could not insist that they do so. The Constitutional documents permitted a club of all one gender. Never in the world did the old guys realize that a one gender club meant that the gender could be "all women" clubs. And many were chartered. That was a difficult adjustment time in Rotary.

I recall at a charter night when we were inducting a new Club of about half men and half women members. Each new member stood up and said something about joining Rotary.

One young lady stood up and said: "I am so pleased to become a Rotarian. My father was a long time Rotarian and he used to take my brother and me to the Rotary picnic, the Rotary Christmas Party and the Rotary

District conference. He has passed away now, but he would be so pleased to know that one of his children is now a Rotarian. But, he would be absolutely appalled to know which one!"

One club president told me that they had a member who said, "If you bring a woman member into this club, I'm out of here." So, they did bring a woman member into the club, and sure enough, the guy resigned. About 6 months later, the fellow showed up at the Club meeting for a make-up. The President said, "Why are you here?" The fellow said, "Well, I joined the morning Club." The President said, "Well, don't they have some women members?" And the visitor responded, "Yeah, and you know, it's kind of nice!"

So, gradually, Club after Club began to invite community and business leaders. In seven years, the minimum time it takes for a Rotarian to become a District Governor, we had our first 8 women District Governors in 1995–96. This year, 2014, 84 Districts will have women District Governors.

And next year, 2015, three women will be serving on the international Board.

I am the first to admit that this may seem to be a very slow process of absorption of women Rotarians into the top leadership of Rotary. But, I am sure it will not be too long before Rotary can point to our first female world President.

This transition has been an extremely significant one for the actual existence of Rotary International. It is estimated that approximately 20% of all the Rotarians in the world are now women. In an organization of 1.2 million members, we are fortunate to have about 240,000 women members. Without women members, Rotary International would not have the membership growth; nor be the highly recognized association throughout the world it is today.

Not only do women members make up a significant segment of our total membership, I suspect that the addition of women into Rotary has reduced the average age of Rotarians by 40 years!

Beyond the equality factor, leadership and the membership numbers, women have added a few other changes to Rotary. Perhaps there is just a little more dignity, respect and courtesy shown in traditional Rotary meetings. Although I have always expected Rotary meetings to be dignified, I suspect that some men are just a little more reserved in their choice of language and stories when women are sitting at the tables.

However, I might say, when our Rotary Club has its annual "joke-athon meeting" some of raunchiest jokes seem to come from our female members!

And another change I've seen since women came into Rotary: when a Rotary Club is planning a special celebration or a District Conference, the very first item on the agenda is now—"what type of centerpieces will we have on the tables." I don't remember the guys *ever* having that on their agenda.

Another personal observation I have had is that since we have had women members, things seem to get done just a little faster. In those previous years, if a job didn't seem to get done, we would say, "Well, ol' Charlie will get around to doing it. But you know Charlie."

Not anymore! Now our women leaders say, "You have 2 days to get that done, or I'll get Jane to do it and she'll have it done in an hour."

Men aren't really procrastinators—they are just a little more *understanding*.

One other change I've noticed since women became Rotarians, after the meeting, when we just had guys; there was never a line up in front of the restroom.

And finally, another major difference I've seen since women have entered Rotary is that it is now possible to induct a new member into your Rotary Club and receive a little kiss or a hug—and nobody looks "funny" at you.

So, on this 25th Anniversary of the first women members in Rotary I salute all the female Rotarians who have added so much to Rotary International. Rotary is alive and thriving because of the contributions of women Rotarians. To all the women today, I commend you for being Rotarians.

One final thought—we must never forget, it was *men* who voted to bring women into Rotary!

The following are comments from District 5300 PDG Steve Garrett. Steve introduced me to many of the RI presidents I have met, and he was a mentor to our small club. He possesses a vast amount of information about Rotary.

The Arrival of the Relief Column

There is something to be said for longevity and proximity to provide perspective on events. When the men of the Rotary Club of Duarte made a decision to invite a few ladies to join their group I was a member of the neighboring Rotary Club of Arcadia and it was my club who had originally worked to create and charter the Rotary Club of Duarte in 1952.

As the original sponsors for the Duarte club my fellow Rotarians in Arcadia made the decision to provide legal and financial support to right a perceived wrong by Rotary International. That led to the ironic circumstance where a member of the Rotary Club of Arcadia, John Fee, was serving as the district governor when the Supreme Court ruled against Rotary International in May of 1987 to bring the Rotary Club of Duarte back into the good graces and full membership in Rotary International. So I was a part of the group that started this process, fueled the process of change and happy celebrant when the process came to fruition.

It was probably a reasonable decision to make Rotary an all-male organization at the inception in 1905. That reasonable policy, like many turn of the century policies should have changed with the times over the next seventy years. The risk of failure of a great organization like Rotary lies in the idea that we always did it that way and there is no reason to question the basic reasoning of a policy the ultimately challenges the very existence of the organization. The reasonableness of the original policy disappeared at some point before Richard Keyes invited the first woman to join the Rotary Club of Duarte and that point was probably a lot closer in proximity to the original charter in 1952 than the restoration of the charter in 1987.

What were we, in our collective wisdom thinking during all of those years to put the future success of Rotary in jeopardy? I have often told the story of my querying old time Rotarians on what justified our intransigence in recognizing the need for adapting to changing circumstances. Why were we challenging the admonition that the alternative to adapting and evolving was withering and ultimately perishing?

The humorous answer to that provocative question is that we were afraid of what would happen to our time honored tradition of opening a weekly meeting with a joke; and sure enough the arrival of women in our midst has led to raunchier joke telling. Another reason for opposing women in our midst was the predictable demand by those with more aesthetic sensibilities that we replace our plastic table cloths with real linen ones and real centerpieces must be added to the salt and pepper shakers. Most distressing to me was the inevitable nutritional trade-off of desserts for healthy salads. The greatest opposition to change was a gnawing fear that out eighty-year tradition of self-congratulation over relatively minor successes would be challenged by increased pressure to do more, do better and have greater vision of what we should be doing.

It is the last fear of the unknown that has proven to be the greatest benefit to the world's oldest and best service organization. With added resources of wallets, hands and minds Rotary has grown in both membership and vision. We are tackling bigger challenges and accomplishing more than we ever would by limiting our membership to half the available candidates. The women of Rotary are not really better persons; they are simply people with a different perspective and different experiences. They don't just add to our capabilities; they multiply what we can accomplish in a pursuit of service above self.

It is all well and good to see the wisdom of adapting rather than perishing. It is reassuring to know that we certainly wouldn't repeat our past failure in the world of today. Reassuring yes, but we are repeating past errors in new ways. The same myopia regarding the opportunity of inviting women to join our ranks exist in our failure to reach out to younger people, people of different ethnicity and background. We, as an organization and as individuals, need to break the habit of limiting our vision of possible members to our own small circle of friends. If the development of acquaintances as an opportunity for service (the first Object of Rotary) is what we really believe in then we need to develop some new different acquaintances. We need to learn from our past mistakes and expand our horizons or success will be in jeopardy; our very existence will be in jeopardy.

July, 2014

The following is a piece entitled "Remembering the Battle of Women Coming into Rotary," written by Frank J. Devlyn, past president of Rotary International, 2000–01.

I am proud to have this opportunity to share some personal history related to Women Coming Into The Family of Rotary Clubs in which Sylvia V. Whitlock, PDG 2012–2013 of District 5300 always likes to remind me that I am one of those highly responsible for this to have happened.

It just happens that during the Council of Legislation in 1989 when this subject was discussed, I was the last delegate representing my District 4170 of Mexico given the opportunity to speak in support of women coming into Rotary. The then Board of directors of R.I. under the leadership of President Royce Abbey was highly supportive of having women coming to Rotary, but it was necessary to get a 2/3 majority of the total number of votes coming from the delegates from all the world of Rotary to be in favor. This was necessary to make the necessary changes in our official documents which would allow Rotary Clubs to admit qualified women for club membership in the same way that men were accepted. I have the honor as Sylvia mentions that my "inspiring, forceful and most sincere comments" as those of other delegates including the importance of Past, Present Senior R.I. Leaders helped many of the delegates from developed and developing countries vote in favor of Women Coming Into Rotary.

I have to admit that I personally have always been an admirer of outstanding women found in the professional, academic and business world. In that 1988 R.I. Council of Legislation we were able to hear enlightening comments from the elected R.I. delegates coming from all parts of the world who were for or against women coming into Rotary. All these comments, reasoning, etc. was considered from the delegates who lined up to speak for and against like those also coming from other present and past Rotary Senior Leaders who attended that Historic Council of Legislation. Without a doubt, women coming into Rotary officially was one subject way overdue.

I had participated in 2 other councils of legislation before this historic 1989 council of legislation. Women coming into Rotary had been steadily getting more votes at every Council of Legislation where I had also spoken in favor of women coming into Rotary when I was still not a member of the R.I. Board. I recall that in the Council of Legislation of 1986 a majority were in favor of women coming into Rotary, but we needed a 2/3 majority to change our official documents.

It is important to remember that the U.S. Supreme Court had made a ruling that women could not be prohibited from joining organizations such as Rotary in the U.S.A. That ruling did not have to be respected in the other 180 plus countries and geographical areas of the World of Rotary. It is important to bring out that Rotary International is a worldwide organization and the customs and cultures vary from country to country. In fact we find that customs and cultures vary in those same countries similar to what we find in the U.S.A. where the majority in the South are different from the majority in the North, etc.

The role of women like other minority groups has always been an uphill battle in all countries of the world. Unfortunately there are cultures where they still think that the role of the women should be quite different to that of men, using all kind of reasoning. We have to remember that all minorities in all parts of the world have always had to have those initial leaders at all levels who Stand Up to Create Awareness to Take Action in making all see that necessary changes have to occur where equality has to be given to all.

In Rotary that initial leader was Past District Governor Sylvia V. Whitlock. Sylvia in this book will relate how her Duarte Rotary Club of California faced an uphill battle with Ups & Downs in getting district, zone and international acceptance for allowing qualified women to be accepted into Rotary Clubs. The work of Sylvia and her Duarte Rotary Club stands out because they did not "throw in the towel" as others had done.

Sylvia Whitlock led the "Good Rotary Fight" which helped make it possible to change things in Rotary. She joined with others to remind the World of Rotary that we are a well-recognized international organization and that Rotary had always changed with the times. It took a Leader like Sylvia to stand up with her colleagues and question the leadership of R.I. as to why qualified women had not been accepted previously. Sylvia, having an Afro-American background, was a person who knew all too well what it meant and why it was necessary to "Fight For Your Rights."

On a personal note I have to bring out that my mother Dr. Nelva Devlyn, was the first woman optometrist in Mexico in the late 30's and early 40's. In the early 60's she was later named "woman of the year" in our hometown Juarez, Chihuahua-Mexico, a border city with El Paso, Texas a city of over 1.8 million persons. She worked alongside my father Dr. Frank J. Devlyn and was a very successful professional and business woman. She truly stood out among men and women as had my father. When she was 90 years of age she was named Senior Woman of

The Year for Juarez, Chihuahua-Mexico. After women were admitted to Rotary, she had also been named an Honorary Rotarian from 2 of the 14 Rotary Clubs of our hometown city which borders with the U.S.A. city of El Paso, Texas.

I am glad to remind all that Rotary like other successful businesses, enterprises, schools, governments, churches, civil organizations, etc. has always changed with the times to serve as an example to the world.

Thank you Sylvia V. Whitlock for your leadership role in this important change which has served as an example for other organizations like the above mentioned.

Without a doubt, Rotary today is all the better for women coming into Rotary.

VIVA ROTARY!

Lyn Kenney is a Rotarian who thinks it is important to document the journeys of women who were breaking the glass ceiling of male-only membership in Rotary. She sent the following text to me about her efforts to make a videotape project about Women in Rotary.

In 2010, two years prior to the 25th anniversary of Women in Rotary, or Women of Rotary as some prefer to say, I started focusing on the general history of women that had been part of Rotary since 1910. This search led to amazing contacts all over the world and a collection of pictures and stories that few Rotarians knew about. A power point presentation was prepared, with assistance from Sandra Duckworth and the Rotary Global History Fellowship (RGHF)

While collecting this information, I realized we had a number of women that were "firsts" on the Rotary scene and I wanted to hear their stories. Sylvia Whitlock was the first person officially to become the first woman President of a Rotary club. There were eight "first" women District Governors in 1994. I decided to interview all of them and do a videotape so that their visual history would not be lost to Rotarians in years to come. My first attempt took place in New Orleans at the Rotary International Convention. This was followed by inviting Sylvia and the seven women PDG's (one—Mimi Altman is deceased) to present at the District 7750 Conference in Savannah. Sylvia gave a keynote speech, and a panel discussion took place with Sylvia and five of the seven women that attended. This was videotaped along with individual video tapes and posted on RGHF.

The women all placed emphasis on being a "Rotarian" and not their status of a Woman in Rotary. They shared wonderful stories of breaking the barrier that existed among some Rotarians that were not pleased with women entering their ranks. In the history I present from 1910, I have repeatedly stated that we all need to remember the time and events throughout history that shaped the thinking of men that were Rotarians. They took a stand that was no different than other all-male social and business clubs. Many of these years women did not even have the right to vote!

It took one more year and some travel to reach the last two PDG's to be interviewed and videotaped. During that process, I also interviewed Mimi Altman's daughter (same name as her mother and active in Rotary) and the first woman Executive Director of Rotary to be made a

Rotarian following the court case. In Mimi's video, she talks about her mother being bounced, as a baby, on the knee of Paul Harris.

The project did not seem complete until I included the "first" women who were on the Foundation Board, the "firsts" to be Directors and Officers, and the first woman, Nan McCreadle, to be President of Rotary International in the British Isles (RIBI). I never guessed it would have been so difficult to coordinate times and places to meet. Then it became apparent that their history had not yet been written. It is difficult to be candid about your office and share stories when you are still in the position. After several years have passed, I hope someone picks up where I left off and videotapes interviews with these incredible women. This is a part of documented history that should not be lost.

My passion for the history of Women in Rotary continues. I found it sad that there was only one picture of the first eight women District Governors which appeared on the cover of the RI magazine in the Netherlands. There is no picture that I have seen of the "Seattle 15." The women that went into the Seattle International Club as a group to defy the stand against women in Rotary. Maybe someone will read this and go through their albums and come up with historical pictures that may be posted for all to see. Sylvia's Rotary Club of Duarte was only a trailblazer. Often referred to as "The Mouse That Roared," it led to my closing statement in presenting the History of Women in Rotary. As Doug Rudman, one of the charter members of Rotary Global History Fellowship, stated, "If you build a better mousetrap, the world will beat a path to your door. Rotary is a better mousetrap. It is time we started treating it that way."

Sylvia Whitlock

*PRIVP Anne L. Matthews was in attendance at the 2012 Internatiᵥ ıal
Assembly, where I was given the opportunity to address the Rotary world's
governors elect. We were seated together at one of the sessions. She was kind
enough to send me the following:*

In 1989, I was invited by three clubs in Columbia, South
Carolina to join Rotary. I joined Columbia East because
it was a smaller club, (48 at that time, as I recall) and it
was where my minister was a member. He had invited
me to join his club. I was the first woman member. Some
of the men were very gracious and welcomed me. A few
were ambivalent but that was natural at that particular
time. That attitude never bothered me, as I knew in
time I would be accepted and I was. I was given work
immediately and I enjoyed doing everything because it
gave me an opportunity to learn all aspects at the club
level. I became the president three years later and after
that served in many positions. All the roles have been
rewarding and meaningful.

There were no women in Rotary for me to model in
1989. I felt I needed to ask other women to join and I
did. Not only did these women join my club, but some
joined other clubs. I was pleased with these additions.
At times, this process required "extra" communication
on my part, as there were men who still were hesitant in
having women members.

I can truthfully say I have had no problems with men in
any of my roles in Rotary. I grew up with five brothers
and I learned team building techniques at an early age
and how to win and lose with dignity and grace. I played
sports with my brothers and competed in games. Life is
a game, regardless of the territory one is working in, and

if one learns how to play the game with integrity and earnestness, all goes well in most cases.

Since I was asked to write about women issues, my experiences, and hopes, I need to state that my Mother and one high school business teacher were the WOMEN role models in my life. My Mother was my greatest fan, telling me often that I could do or be anything I wanted in life, as long as I believed I could succeed and if I were willing to work hard. She instilled in me, as did my Dad, a strong self work ethic. The high school business teacher was a professional and a Southern lady whom I adored. I wanted to be just like her "when I became a teacher." Both taught me skills, social graces, and appropriate behavior that I have used wisely in every position in my career and in my personal life.

Above, I stated I was the first president of my club. I also was the first woman governor in D7770, a large Rotary district in South Carolina with 78 clubs and 5,000 members in 1999–2000. I worked hard and with my team, we raised the bar in every aspect of Rotary. I placed women on the team and they certainly added value to everything we attempted that year. We were acknowledged at the Zones 33 and 34 Institute as having the greatest increase in all areas of The Rotary Foundation.

I was appointed the first woman Regional Rotary Foundation Coordinator (RRFC) for Zone 33 and we broke records, with the help of a lot of capable people, including several women. I was elected by the RI Board in 2009 to serve as a Foundation Trustee, beginning in 2010, the second woman to be elected a trustee. There were no other women trustees during the two years I served. I was, shortly thereafter, elected to serve as a director for Zones 33 and 34, the first woman elected to this role in these zones. Candidly, there was pressure from one senior leader for me to resign immediately from the trustee position, since I had been elected to serve as the director beginning in 2012.

During one of our trustee meetings, the trustees discussed the situation, took a vote and the vote was unanimous for me to remain as a trustee for the full two years and not to resign. All along, senior leaders had come to me and asked me not to resign. That was a vote I shall value and cherish all my life. I worked well with all of the trustees and I believe they valued the contributions I made as a trustee. After serving two years as a trustee, I resigned effective June 30, 2012, and started serving as a director July 1, 2012. (A precedent had already been established as others before me had served as a trustee, had been elected to serve as a director, and had resigned at the end of the two-year period, so I really was following the precedent that had been established.)

In early 2013, President-Elect Ron Burton asked me to serve as his vice president during the 2013–14 year, and I was elected by his Board. He and I had served together on the Future Vision Committee for several years, and we knew each other well. I was highly honored, as this would be the first time a woman would serve as vice president of Rotary International. It was a wonderful experience serving with President Ron and the Board members. Truly, it was a great year that I shall always remember.

Since this is a narrative on women issues and some of my experiences in Rotary, for the record, I was the first woman elected to serve both as a trustee of The Rotary Foundation and as a member of the Rotary International Board of Directors.

I have had the opportunity to meet and work side by side with both male and female Rotarians in locations all over the world and have become great friends with many. Women have been kind, supportive, and very encouraging. We have made progress in Rotary, even though it has been slow. It takes competence, hard work, people skills, a thick skin, staying focused, professionalism, and hope. I believe male Rotarians will one day recognize that women are as capable as men to serve in any role in Rotary and that professional women should be provided the opportunity to do so. As one PDG stated to me in the mid-west, "Anne, women make Rotary! Rotary would be in deep trouble without them." And he was sincere. It took twenty five years, since the formal acceptance of women in Rotary, (thanks to Dr. Sylvia Whitlock and others in CA) for a woman to become the vice president. We need open-minded, professional Rotarians like PRIP President Ron Burton, who selects individuals based on valid credentials and not gender. One day soon, this will happen! I have faith! Let's keep hope and prayers at our forefront and it will happen!

I am most grateful for Rotary. It has given me much more than I have given it and I shall continue to serve in any way I can to help the less fortunate in the world. I am blessed.

I have had the honor to address or participate in the International Assembly, international conventions, Rotary institutes, district conferences, Foundation events, celebratory events, and club meetings on the subject of women in Rotary. I have never turned down an invitation to speak and have broken only one commitment—because of a funeral. I have always thought that if people are interested enough in hearing what I have to say, the least I can do is try my best to make it happen. I have spoken at events in Oranjestad, Aruba; Melbourne, Australia; Cape Town, South Africa; Clapham, London, England; Aberdeen, Scotland; Kingston, Jamaica; Nassau, Bahamas; Tijuana, Mexico; and Vancouver, Washington. I have traveled to Texas, Florida, South Carolina, North Carolina, Minnesota, Missouri, Kentucky, Oregon, Washington, Nevada, and numerous clubs throughout the state of California, from the desert to the ocean and everywhere north and south. These experiences have all helped me to see Rotary at its best and most varied.

Following are copies of speeches I have been asked to make available. One of them, which I gave during the 2013 International Assembly, is available from Rotary International. Several, I have noticed, can be found on YouTube.

One group that I know, Rotary Global History Fellowship—chaired now by Jack Selway but with whom my initial contact was Doug Rudman, who invited me to speak in Texas—and one person I know, Lyn Kenney, have both been proactive in securing the history of women in Rotary for our archives.

The following is a speech I gave in January 2013 at the International Assembly in San Diego, California, at the invitation of PRIP Ron Burton.

Diversity in Rotary

Never judge someone by the way he looks
Or a book by the way it is covered
For inside the tattered pages
There's a lot to be discovered

From my grandmother, I learned, "Never judge a book by its cover," but only really understood that phrase when I had a significant, thought-altering experience many years ago. I was raised in a third-world culture where class distinctions were the rule of the day and the main earmarks of prejudice. Because I was a light-skinned black person, I thought myself immune to the pronunciations of worthlessness heaped on darker-skinned persons. As a young person, unschooled in the etymology of the black race, my response to differences were largely only skin-deep. One of the insidious consequences of prejudice is that you can be taught to undervalue and fear, even hate, those of whom you are really a part. In a musical commentary on life in the '40s, Rodgers and Hammerstein wrote *South Pacific*. Hear a part of the words of Rogers and Hammerstein's "You've Got to Be Carefully Taught," written and scored by Rodgers and Hammerstein:

You've got to be taught to hate and fear.
You've got to be taught from year to year.
It's got to be drummed in your dear little ear.
You've got to be carefully taught.

So my soul-searching moment came when I ran out of gasoline on a busy New York City expressway, and my car sputtered to a halt in the fast lane, where there was no shoulder. I walked ahead to the police phone to report my plight and was told by the person on the other end of the line, "If you're still there in an hour, call us back." As I stood there befuddled, a car going in the other direction on the other side of the freeway pulled up, and the driver, a black man with his head tied by a ragged handkerchief, called out, "What's the matter, baby?" I can't adequately describe for you the hesitation with which I explained my problem, because I was looking right at the cover of this man, and it was everything I had been taught to avoid. He said, "I'll get you some gas, baby," and in the ten minutes or so before he returned, a million unpleasant scenarios played in my head. He returned, poured gasoline from a can into the gas tank, poured some on the carburetor, and started my car. I offered to give him the three dollars I had with me, but he refused it, saying it cost him only twenty-nine cents—remember, this was in the 1960s! I went on my way—I was only about ten minutes from home—went inside and took a deep breath to reconstruct what had just happened. What had just happened was that I had found inside some tattered pages a gem! I replayed the potentially dangerous situation—stranded on the freeway—and realized it was that concern for my safety that led me to believe in a seemingly undesirable quality. I dug deeply to find the genesis of those beliefs which had excluded this man from my circle of acceptables. It is a journey we must all take, hopefully without the push of a precarious situation.

When I was invited to join the Rotary Club of Duarte, which was, at the time, engaged in a court struggle over the admission of women, I learned about the place to which many women were relegated—in the minds of men *and* women! We received a few gender-based, unpleasant telephone calls, and I found myself wondering anew about the deep-seated beliefs that were leading many to reject the idea that women could be capable Rotarians. Had we looked around, we would have seen, as PRI president Magiyagbe described it, women working alongside men in almost every area of employment—as physicians, as professors, as engineers, as construction workers, as business executives. When the first Rotary bylaws were written, they specified that Rotarians should be "persons of integrity." Somehow, that morphed into "men." What then was the genesis of that belief—that women were not worthy of or capable of being Rotarians and working to provide the same humanitarian assistance that men were doing? It may not even have been a relegation of women to a place of lesser importance and value but may have been a belief that women could and would not do the heavy work that needed to be done—or I would like to believe that some men were so invested in the valor of their commitment to Rotary, they did not want to share it with women.

Either way, the result is that a part of our society excluded, without good reason, another part deemed incapable of sharing their exploits. We have learned, from the presence of women in Rotary, that they are capable of much more than "behind-the-scenes meal preparation," as one caller suggested. Interestingly enough, most of the great chefs are male! Is it as Clare Booth Luce said? "Because I am a woman, I must make unusual efforts to succeed. If I fail, no one will say, 'She doesn't have what it takes.' They will say, 'Women don't have what it takes.'" But they do—they can and do work alongside men, bringing their mystique to the board tables, the work trenches, the financial negotiations, and all of the parts that men and women have been so successful in doing for the past twenty-five years. Yes, there is a gender perspective, but it is not a conflict-producing perspective. Susan B. Anthony said, "The day will come when man will recognize woman as his peer, not only at the fireside, but in the councils of the nations. Then, and not until then will there be the perfect comradeship, the ideal union between the sexes, that shall result in the highest development of the race." We need to take time to look deep inside us to find where our biases originate and how we extinguish them. Younger generations are more accepting, because we have taught them, even if we don't practice it ourselves, that there is only a common humanity whose generosity is not segmented by race, creed, color, gender, age, or sexual preference. Are we there yet?

What about the ethnic diversity?

Margaret Mead, the renowned anthropologist, said, "If we are to achieve a richer culture, rich in contrasting values, we must recognize the whole gamut of human potentialities, and so weave a less arbitrary social fabric, one in which each diverse gift will find a fitting place." In many countries, we have a de facto segregation of races, yet in many, we do not, and Rotary meetings seem to be peopled by persons more alike than diverse. As we grow a new generation used to sharing their space with people of different colors, different genders, and different sexual persuasions, we can expect to see not just a tolerance but a spirit of inclusion toward people of different persuasions, whose common goal is service above self. Isabel Allende said, "Peace requires everyone to be in the circle—each one to contribute to its wholeness, inclusion." Mahnaz Afkhami, a lifelong advocate of human rights, said, "We have the ability to achieve, if we master the necessary goodwill, a common global society, blessed with a shared culture of peace that is nourished by the ethnic, national and local diversities that enrich our lives." We are no longer small residential communities; our community is the world.

We are here today, in this place, a community of more than five hundred districts, as diverse a group as we could ever imagine, and we will walk out of here with friends from places we hardly knew anything about. *We are the world.* We cannot replace hate and fear with apathy toward others with whom we smile and for whom we do not hesitate to serve but will not walk alongside. Service engenders self-pride, and why should we deny those opportunities to others? We can help them to help themselves by encouraging them to fish along with us. Michael Jackson sang, about the world, "Make a little space. Make it a better place. Heal the world. Peace is our goal. Let's start within our hearts! We are the world."

The following is a speech I presented at a zone institute in Kentucky and revised for 2014 Southern California and Nevada PETS.

Sylvia Whitlock

Diversity in Rotary

Distinguished Rotarians, president elects, and guests, thank you for inviting me to talk with you about diversity and Rotary membership—how embracing one helps the other. I will share with you some of the experiences significant to our Rotary journeys and some of the life lessons I have learned. Incoming president Gary Huang says, "Light up Rotary."

RI President Ron Burton asks us to "engage Rotary, change lives." The lives you change will include your own. Let me tell you a little of how Rotary changed my life in the process of service above self, the learning and opportunities for growth.

I have had twenty-seven years to learn about this institution called Rotary International, to feel myself a functional part of this great humanitarian organization, probably the greatest—certainly the largest—of the humanitarian organizations we know. There are many service organizations that we know. But I had the good fortune to be invited, by a far-seeing Rotarian, to join the all-male Rotary Club of Duarte. He took a chance to invite women, because he was invested in the possibilities that could come with a larger club. When I was invited to join the Rotary Club of Duarte, which was, at the time, engaged in a court struggle over the admission of women, I learned about the place to which many women were relegated—in the minds of men *and* women. There were many *women* who opposed the admission of women, and believe it or not, I met some of them in India a few months ago—a stalwart group of Rotary Anns! As we made our eleven-year journey through California courts, we received a few gender-based, unpleasant telephone calls, and I found myself wondering about the deep-seated beliefs that were leading many to reject the idea that women could be capable Rotarians—as volunteers serving from the heart. Had we looked around, we would have seen, as past RI president Magiyagbe described it, women working alongside men in almost every area of employment—as physicians, as professors, as engineers, as construction workers, as business executives. When the first Rotary bylaws were written, they specified that Rotarians should be "persons of integrity." Somehow, at a time when there were more men than women in the management positions of the workaday world, that morphed into "men." It wasn't tested until women were invited to join Rotary, and then the uproar resulted in the recall of the charter of the Duarte club. What then was the genesis of that belief, outside of the bylaws, that women were not worthy of or capable of being Rotarians and working to provide the same humanitarian assistance that men were doing? It may not even have been a relegation of women to a place of lesser importance and value but may have been a belief that women couldn't shoulder the work that needed to be done—or I would like to believe that some men were so invested in the valor of their commitment to Rotary, they did not want to share it with women.

Either way, the result is that a part of our society excluded, without good reason, another part deemed incapable of sharing their exploits. We have learned, from the presence of women in Rotary, that they are capable of much more than "behind-the-scenes meal preparation," as one caller suggested. Interestingly enough, most of the great chefs are male! Is it as Clare Booth Luce said? "Because I am a woman, I must make unusual efforts to succeed. If I fail, no one will say, 'She doesn't have what it takes.' They will say, 'Women don't have what it takes.'" There are still clubs today that say they cannot find Rotary-caliber women. A few weeks ago, in Victoria, British Columbia, a past president told me that fourteen male members resigned when he invited women to join his club. He says they were replaced and their duties assumed by four women. You see, they do—they can and do work alongside men, bringing their mystique to the board tables, the work trenches, the financial negotiations, and all of the parts that men and women have been so successful in doing for the past twenty-five years. Yes, there is a gender perspective, but it is not a conflict-producing perspective. Susan B. Anthony said, "The day will come when man will recognize woman as his peer, not only at the fireside, but in the councils of the nations. Then, and not until then will there be the perfect comradeship, the ideal union between the sexes, that shall result in the highest development of the race." What are some of the other situations that tend to limit our access to capable Rotarians?

Never judge someone by the way he looks
Or a book by the way it is covered
For inside the tattered pages
There's a lot to be discovered!

From my grandmother, I learned, "Never judge a book by its cover," but only really understood that phrase when I had a significant, thought-altering experience many years ago. I was raised in a third-world culture where class distinctions were the rule of the day and the main earmarks of prejudice. Because I was a light-skinned black person, I thought myself immune to the pronunciations of worthlessness heaped on darker-skinned persons. As a young person, unschooled in the etymology of the black race, my response to differences were largely only skin-deep. One of the insidious consequences of prejudice is that you can be taught to undervalue and fear, even disdain, those of whom you are really a part. As a musical commentary on life in the '40s, Rodgers and Hammerstein wrote *South Pacific*. Following are part of the song's words. If you know the story, it is sung during the scene in which the young Lieutenant Cable is being courted by Bloody Mary as a husband for her Polynesian daughter. He is told by a colleague that his reluctance comes from something with which he was born. He disagrees, in the words of the following song:

You've got to be carefully taught.
You've got to be taught before it's too late,
Before you are six or seven or eight.

So my soul-searching moment came when I ran out of gasoline on a busy New York City expressway, and my car sputtered to a halt in the fast lane, where there was no shoulder. I walked ahead to the highway-patrol phone to report my problem and was told by the person on the other end of the line, "If you're still there in an hour, call us back." As I stood there, befuddled and probably looking very pathetic, a car going in the other direction on the other side of the freeway pulled up, and the driver, a black man with his head tied by a ragged handkerchief, called out, "What's the matter, baby?" I can't adequately describe for you the hesitation with which I explained my problem, because I was looking right at the cover of this man, and it was everything I had been taught to avoid. He said, "I'll get you some gas, baby," and in the ten minutes or so before he returned, a million unpleasant scenarios played in my head. He returned, poured gasoline from a can into the gas tank, poured some on the carburetor, and started my car. I offered to give him the three dollars I had with me, but he refused it, saying it cost him only twenty-nine cents—remember, this was in the 1960s! I went on my way—I was only about ten minutes from home—went inside and took a deep breath to reconstruct what had just happened. What had just happened was that I had found inside some tattered pages a gem! I replayed the potentially dangerous situation—stranded on the freeway—and realized it was that concern for my safety that led me to trust in a seemingly undesirable quantity. I dug deeply to find the genesis of *my* beliefs, which had excluded this man from my circle of acceptables. It is a journey we should all take, hopefully without the push of a precarious situation.

Today, I look back at the naiveté of my thinking then. Should I have been concerned about his appearance, over which he had little control, or over his behavior, over which he has the ultimate control? A few weeks ago, I had occasion to change planes in Portland Airport. I was getting off a toy plane—express planes, they call them—and transferring to a full-size airplane, so the walk between the terminals was long. I was tired and lazy and had a bag whose wheels were as challenged as my knees, so I requested a wheelchair. As we taxied to the gate, I could see the wheelchair being managed by someone who appeared learning challenged. Now, I'm an educator, and I have worked with students who were educable and students who were trainable, and my own personal ethics, even without the Four-Way Test, prescribe my behavior. But in my head, I was thinking, *I hope he can find the way to the other terminal.* It didn't take five seconds for my better brain to kick in and say, *What are you thinking? What is your problem?* I watched the young man navigate through a number of back hallways, up and down elevators, over some pretty rough terrain that he could have and should have avoided, and over the journey, my appreciation of the fact that he was holding a job, and doing it well, continued to grow. At my destination, I gave him twice the gratuity I would ordinarily have given—part of it genuinely for him but the other part to assuage my guilt at questioning his appearance and doubting his ability because of it. Can someone with Down's syndrome be a good Rotarian? Think about it for a while. So I continue to negotiate the journey through Rotary.

So where has this journey with Rotary taken me?

To Kentucky, for one. I have not traveled much in the southern United States, and much of what I have has been for Rotary. I have attended meetings, as makeups, in the London Clapham Club, where a female was as much diversity as they could handle, and they toasted me on the same glass of champagne on which they toasted the queen. One of my more significant events was traveling to India to be part of the NIDS team. I grew up in a country that was part of the British Commonwealth, as was India. But the India of my history books was the India of elephant walk and maharajas and magnificent palaces. I was not prepared for the squalor and poverty I saw in many of the parts of India where we traveled to give polio inoculations. But I was also not prepared for the contrast in lifestyles present in that huge populace. I was also not prepared for the size of the hearts in Indian Rotarians, their dogged pursuit of solutions to health and education needs—look at their record in polio—their graciousness and hospitality, their sense of responsibility toward changing economic and social situations in their country. My governor's project this past year was to raise money for a school in India, a school devoted to the education of girls—all first-generation learners—started by an Indian woman who came to America when she was a teenager. She is addressing another aspect of exclusion and providing for the diversity of learners. Nicholas Kristoff, in his award-winning book *Half the Sky*, addresses the victimization of women around the world, including our own United States. One effort toward erasing that victimization is the education of girls, who will pass on that goal to their children and their children's children.

I have engaged Rotary in many ways. It has encouraged me to focus on the fact that we, both you and I, need to take time to look deep inside us to find where our biases originate, whether they make sense, whether they are resulting in unethical behavior, and how we extinguish them. *We are, each of us, born with only two sets of unchangeable attributes, and one is still up for question— one is our race, and the other is our gender.* When Sebastian Cruz sang the national anthem a few months ago in one of the NBA final games, racists twittered about the appearance of a Mexican singing the national anthem. Sebastian was born in San Antonio—American born and bred. He was a good singer—a good-looking kid with no apparent objectionable characteristics. What was the valid reason for the objections? Should you even object to someone who wants to sing the national anthem? When my daughter was sixteen and attending youth group in the First Baptist Church, she came home and told me she wanted to be baptized. Well, I had done my duty as a Christian mother and had had her baptized as an infant in the Presbyterian church to which her dad belonged. Well, it wasn't really a baptism; it was a christening—a sprinkling of water—but this was going to be the real thing: baptism by immersion. So somewhat miffed at the fact that my baptism wasn't good enough for her, I went to my minister, seeking his support. His response to me was "Wanting to be baptized can't be the worst thing she ever wanted to do!" So I shut up and put up and happily went to her baptism. So here is a young man, singing the national anthem, doing something positive, and people are asking why. So here was the good and bad. The important thing to remember is, as in the words of the song: "You've got to accentuate the positive, eliminate the negative, latch on to the affirmative."

I try to do my bit to present the picture of blacks in America—and they are perceived differently than blacks from the Caribbean or blacks from Africa—by hosting exchange students whenever I can. Invariably, they leave my home calling me Mom and with a better picture than that with which they entered. I have had students from Germany, Japan, Turkey, and Mexico. I am chosen by people I know, but I am always a surprise to the students. After all, their vision of Americans is largely what they see in the media. For the most part, blacks are not positively presented in the media. But like many other black families, I run a conservative home, I love my family, and we can care for other people's children.

We always eventually get to talking about race relations and perceptions, and I get a chance to demonstrate that everything you see on the cover of a book is not an illustration of its contents. All this is done by engaging Rotary. Hispanics are another vastly misunderstood group, coming as they are from cultures as different as black and white. But their language seems to place them in one group identified as Hispanic.

You *can* raise your children to be color blind.

If we can be taught to hate and fear, we can also be taught to love and appreciate. But it takes some self-awareness that overcomes some inbred biases. When I have a celebration at my home and invite my friends, black is not the predominant color, and I often find myself examining the guest list and wondering why. During one of those celebrations, my daughter was giving a tour through photographs of six years of ballet classes and recitals. In each group of students, she was the only black ballerina. Her challenge to the guest was "Can you find me?" You see, her color was not her identification of herself and, I like to believe, not of anyone else. I have come to learn that the persons who people my world are still the persons who are realizing the advantages with which I grew up. I carry personal guilt because I criticize some of these realities in other people. Sometimes we have to be proactive in reaching out to those who are seldom chosen. Younger generations are more accepting, because we have taught them, even if we don't practice it ourselves, that there is only a common humanity whose generosity is not segmented by race, creed, color, gender, age, or sexual preference We are often put off by the way someone looks—a reaction taught to us by personal, cultural, and social situations. What about the ethnic diversity? Margaret Mead, the renowned anthropologist, said, "If we are to achieve a richer culture, rich in contrasting values, we must recognize the whole gamut of human potentialities, and so weave a less arbitrary social fabric, one in which each diverse gift will find a fitting place."

When I was writing my PhD dissertation, I talked with Gwendolyn Tucker at the University of Michigan, who says, "We do not need a melting pot, but a rich mosaic, where every distinct piece retains its own integrity but contributes to the whole." If we believe in the capability of each piece to contribute something of value, then how rich can we make a club that embraces diversity? In many countries, we have a de facto segregation of races, yet in many, we do not, and Rotary meetings seem to be peopled by persons more alike than diverse. Rotary International says that a club that reflects its community with regards to business and professional classifications, gender, age, religion, and ethnicity is a club with the key to its future. As we grow a new generation used to sharing their space with people of different colors, different genders, and different sexual persuasions, we can expect to see not just a tolerance but a spirit of inclusion toward people of different persuasions whose common goal is service above self. We are working for peace. Isabel Allende said, "Peace requires everyone to be in the circle—each one to contribute to its wholeness, inclusion." Mahnaz Afkhami, a lifelong advocate of human rights, said, "We have the ability to achieve, if we master the necessary goodwill, a common global society, blessed with a shared culture of peace that is nourished by the ethnic, national and local diversities that enrich our lives." Our community is no longer just the residential area in which we live or the town that supports it or the state that governs it. We are citizens of the world, where every issue, no matter how small or seemingly far removed from us, has an effect on us. Our community is the world. Our representatives should resemble the world community. If we are serious about peace and engaging Rotary to change lives, then we must look beyond those shadings of differences that used to dictate how we choose our friends and choose those worthy and capable people who can help us to serve. *We are the world.* We cannot replace hate and fear with apathy toward others with whom we smile and for whom we do not hesitate to serve but will not walk alongside. Service engenders self-pride, and we can build the self-pride of all those engaged in serving others. We can help them to help themselves by encouraging them to fish along with us. Perhaps a good place to start is in the communities we are trying to help. What if we went into those communities and recruited some of their members to help us in our hands-on projects? We're giving them an opportunity to participate in helping themselves, and perhaps, just perhaps, we may find people there, if we are open—people who just might make good Rotarians, who like what we do and would like to work with us. We are humanity; humanitarianism is what we strive to do. Rotary is the best vehicle I know for making that happen. Engage it, and give care, concern, respect, and acceptance. Michael Jackson sang, about the world, "Make a little space. Make it a better place. Heal the world. Peace is our goal. Let's start within our hearts!"

The following is a speech I gave to District 5300 clubs during my year as district governor (2012–13).

In twenty-five years as a bona fide Rotarian, I have heard a lot of governors' speeches—some memorable, some inspirational, some making small blips on my radar screen. So in preparing what I was going to say to you, I had to spend some time thinking about where my passion for Rotary would intersect your interest in being a fulfilled Rotarian. I wanted to speak to you, from my heart, of the events which shaped and continue to shape my Rotary experience.

So where do we start?

I joined the Ex-Rotary Club of Duarte in 1982. I became a Rotarian in 1987, when I attended my first international convention. You see, what I knew about Rotary in those early days of my membership could have been loosely inscribed on the head of a pin. I knew more about Kiwanis (and right here in California, I was told that *Kiwanis* means "waiting to join Rotary") and Elks and Lions—those were stranger-sounding names, but I had quite literally never heard of Rotary until I was invited by the superintendent of schools, Rotarian Richard Key, to join in 1982.

I grew up in Kingston, Jamaica, with my grandparents.

My parents chose not to have their children grow up in the impersonal world of New York City, so we were sent to Jamaica, where we could grow up and revel in our childhood freedoms. I watched my grandmother care for people—the man who worked on the trolley tracks in front of our house; the neighbor who couldn't go down town to Victoria Market; her daughter, who was home with three small children; and so on. She was a kind woman who lived not richly but comfortably, had never heard the words "service above self" but illustrated service above self in her caring, thoughtful way. I have a vivid recollection—super vivid, because for a memory more than sixty-five years old, it must have made quite an impression—of a worker coming to our gate and asking to borrow a fire so he could prepare his lunch. He had, in a small bag, a piece of dried codfish and a piece of yam, staples for poor people. He wanted to just heat it up or steam it for his lunch. She took it from him, cut up some onions and tomatoes, mixed it with some oil, and fixed him a palatable lunch. I remember watching her do this and asking why she did. "Because people will do the same thing for you and your children," she said, "and you just pass it on." You see, she was passing on what she had, because she knew that was the world she wanted to see—sort of paying it forward. She stood on line early in the morning two days each week at the butcher shop to buy meat for her neighbors who couldn't go. She gave me extra sandwiches to take to school for those children who would come to school without lunch. We were not rich or privileged, but we had enough to share—and that's all it is about! So I grew up under that influence, thinking it was natural to do things for people who couldn't do them for themselves, and that mind-set became part of my being. When I started to work, I joined United Way, I gave blood for transfusions regularly, and I tithed in church. How could I have known then that I would later have a child whose life depended on having regular blood transfusions and has for the past thirty-five years? But at that time, the recipients of all of this were faceless people, and the giving was perfunctory. Khalil Gibran said, "It is when you give of yourself that you truly give." The students in my school community were not faceless, and their needs, the community's needs, were palpable. This was what my Rotary club was attending to. We did not participate in international projects, because we were not a real Rotary club. This was what I signed up to do—this was why I spent days collecting used goods for a yard sale or sold snow cones to raise money for classroom libraries or made breakfasts for cancer survivors.

So in 1982, I was invited into one of the most humanitarian-focused organizations in the world—1.2 million strong. I was given the gift of the opportunity to become a service-oriented resident of our planet—a gift larger than life! As I changed from member of the Ex-Rotary Club of Duarte to Rotarian, I came to belong to the body of Rotary—that individual and collective representation of all of us. I have the heart-filling ability, as do you, to address some of the gut-wrenching needs around us. I'd like you to think about the time you were invited to join Rotary and what your expectations were. Chief among them was probably the fact that you were invited by someone you respected, who told you he was giving you an opportunity you couldn't—or shouldn't—refuse!

Volunteers in our organization give with, from, by their hearts. It is the part of the body which pumps up and provides energy to all the other parts. Our hearts, in Rotary, pump through the arteries represented by members, clubs, districts. Looking at our physical bodies, the circulation of blood through the heart is what gives all our organs and extremities the power to act appropriately. The brain is the central processing agency in this body—the director, the vast network that keeps records of all we do and try to do and say. It makes sense of the information we get through our senses and responds appropriately by energizing the other organs. When we hear or see something which touches our hearts, we respond by using our hands to engage in those corrective activities which make the situation better. Our feet take us to the places where we need to be, whether it's to Tecate to build a home for a needy family or to India to assist in the inoculating of children against polio or to Haiti to deliver and set up a shelter box or to New Orleans to support the victims of Katrina or to Hermosillo to distribute wheelchairs or to Costa Rica to participate in Rotoplast. Our bodies respond to the rush of adrenaline, which signals a fight-or-flight situation, and we take action. We respond to the needs wherever they may be with all the gusto our hearts can support.

With every breath we take, we need to spread the word of Rotary.

When I was in New Orleans at a convention a few years ago, we shared the convention hall with a group of microbiologists from across the country and outside the United States. Each day, at least three or four people would ask, "What is Rotary?" and hiding my dismay, I would try to explain in as few words as I could—in my best elevator speech—the magnanimous undertakings of this larger-than-life humanitarian organization. I am still taken aback when I meet people who are now where I was twenty-seven years ago, and I wonder what we can do. Membership increase is on the front burner of goals and objectives at most clubs. Ken Boyd's IGNITE, a program to attract new members to Rotary, is designed to share our caring. We hear countless stories from people who have testified to wearing their pins and sharing what it represents to curious observers. We need to be proactive and to tell our story and to recruit people to help us do the vast amount of work needing to be done. Because we are the world! No longer is our community the residential area in which we live or the town that supports it or even the state that governs it. We are citizens of the world, where every incident, however distant or seemingly far removed, has a ripple effect on us and others. To the extent that they are well, we are well! Let us then go out and spread the word of Rotary and enlist others to help us do the work this world needs. You are only one person, but to the parents of that child into whose mouth you and other Rotarians placed the drops that could save his life, you are the world! How can you be any less?

We do much of this with the help of the Rotary Foundation, which helps us to maximize the funds we raise for world service—first through matching grants and now, in Future Vision, the new look of Rotary grants, through global grants and district grants.

In 2010, we were number four in bequests in the world! In our own zone, I think we were number two. How many times in the last few days or weeks have you seen, heard of, or read about a pressing need in some person's life? That's why we're all in this: because we care, and because we can help. Do you look back at the end of each day and say, "What did I do to help someone today?" Service above self is what we do. Peace through service is our goal. We can make service larger and more sustainable with the help of the Rotary Foundation.

I tell everyone who takes me seriously that I have three children—two wonderful and one not so wonderful!

But I love them all and will divide their inheritance as equally as my conscience, monitored by my brain, will let me. How comforting it will be to know, though (the comfort is now, because I don't think I will know after I am gone, but you know how we like to manage stuff even beyond the grave)—how comforting it will be to know that at least $10,000 of my money, or whatever I will have managed to bequeath before I die, will be spent not on the newest Android or a round-trip expedition to the moon or some electronic equipment that will allow the pool to be heated with a voice command from the bathroom but will be on some clean, safe water for a child to drink or some medical care for his mother, who is suffering from some dread disease, or a family that just needs four walls and a roof to protect them from the elements. So I encourage you to find those painless ways to put some money aside for good causes. When I was a young woman, there was a product called Filter Queen Vacuums sold door-to-door. However, their system to get you to save the money it would take to buy their product was to give you a miniature bank shaped like a vacuum cleaner, into which you would drop a quarter or three dimes every day. All of us could do that, right? Twenty-five cents a day adds up to $91.25 per year. The problem was that you could have a bank for every product you were trying to buy, and pretty soon, that system would be unmanageable. But then, you could choose one that was worth the effort—like PolioPlus. Is that worth our attention? Look at what we've done, you and I! And each and every day, we should say, "What have I done today to help someone or share some of what I have been given?"—even three dimes.

Inspiration that moves us to action:

What is more inspiring than to see a child or adult who had no mobility before smile the wide smile of someone about to take off in a wheelchair? When you gave the keys to their own home to that family in the Corazon build in Tecate, how did you feel? Was it worth the effort? What about the polio victim who can now walk because he has been given prosthetics to replace those limbs ravaged by polio, or the girls who can escape a life of unspeakable victimization because they can now go to school?

We've all read or heard countless stories about people who give their last mite to help someone else. We all have heard about Mother Teresa, who walked the streets of Calcutta to find those who needed food and shelter. We know about Martin Luther King, who literally gave his life because he had a dream, and he would not be dissuaded from it. What we give through Rotary, we give from the bounty with which we have been blessed, and like putting three dimes every day in the Filter Queen bank, we hardly even miss it. But the larger effort, putting our bodies into the work we do, getting our hands dirty to make someone else clean, sacrificing some time to do good work—that is what makes our world a better place, and I don't think there is one person here who doesn't wish a better place for us and our children.

Support

For all of this, I am glad I was invited to be a Rotarian. My desire now is to be of support to all of you who give from the heart.

Here in District 5300, we have a whole cadre of volunteers just like you who have committed to sharing their knowledge of our systems and expertise with you. They can show you how to maximize the dollars you are putting into a project, how to find a project that matches your interests, how to find partners for your projects, how to be part of the Rotary experience around the world. We have been challenged by RI President Tanaka to build peace through service. Our core value is service above self. Help us to help you help the world. Act as if what you do makes a difference! It does!

Encouragement

At the end of this Rotary year, a new president will take the helm of RI. He will introduce a new theme and set some new goals. In District 5300, we will celebrate a successful Rotary year with a conference at the Town and Country Hotel in San Diego. There, we will recognize those of you who have launched exemplary efforts in our goal to serve humanity. We will make your information available to all who wish to replicate your projects. We will celebrate the fun and fellowship that keep us together for a common cause. We will pass the batons on to a new group of leaders who will revitalize and reenergize our spirits. Plan to make attendance at the district conference a major part of your year-end activities, where even there, we will launch a project to benefit one of our neighbor cities. We plan to include activities for youth and children and to have speakers who will more than inspire you. One of them will be Cliff Dochterman.

Just a memory to leave with you: some may remember the pictures I showed when I returned from India.

When I was in India two years ago, the Rotary Club of Calcutta Metropolitan presented an entertainment program in honor of the NIDS team. Brightly dressed in colorful costumes was a troupe of about twenty children, from six to sixteen, who performed some native dances for us. Among the children was an eight-year-old boy who was wearing one shoe with a six-inch platform to make up for a polio-shortened leg. In fact, all of the children were polio survivors who had been taught these dances to bring some joy and laughter into their challenged lives. If all you did was look at the smiling faces of the children who were dancing, you would never have understood the journeys they traveled to this place. But travel they did, in a journey barely begun. Because the Rotary Club of Calcutta Metropolitan has made a commitment to provide lifelong artificial limbs, education, health care, and vocational training to this group of youngsters. This is what Rotarians do. This is what we do. Our goal is to make the world a better place—cleaner, healthier, more self-sustaining, happier, and more peaceful than it was when we came into it. Can we do it? We must.

The following is a message to my District 5300 members in December 2012, Family Month.

It is probably fitting that December should be designated as Family Month in our Rotary year. All around the month of December, we have celebrations and observations that are occasions for family gatherings for our immediate and extended biological families. But as we look around us in the world of Rotary, we must acknowledge those very extended families we create as we go through the business of serving and being served. In my own circle, I have students from Indonesia, Turkey, Mexico, Ecuador, and the Netherlands who continue to call me Mom. They are my family, and I don't love them any less than I do my own children, because together, we have laughed, cried, argued, hugged, and kissed—just as I have with my biological children. Family is not defined by blood lines but by heart lines, and as we crisscross the globe in our search to serve humanity in all the myriad ways that Rotarians do, we create families in many places—in our meeting rooms, in our service projects, in the homes we share here and abroad, and in the relationships that bring lasting, meaningful memories. My class of governors this year is my family, as I so readily realized when I saw them all in Squaw Valley a week ago. We share a common purpose, we are nurtured by the Rotary beliefs we espouse, and we will forever be family by virtue of the links established this year. As you begin to plan holiday patties, make them family friendly and acknowledge that basic building block of all humanity: the family! We plan to make our district conference a family event. In that most comfortable of places, where we strive to find unconditional acceptance, we can do no better than to widen our circle and draw into it all who need forgiveness, acceptance, warmth, and nurture. Celebrate your families this month—all of them—and then, next month, start all over again!

Happy holidays to my Rotary family!

THIS HAS BEEN MY FIRST-PERSON RECOLLECTION OF THE INCIDENTS WITH which I was involved and of the routes through which they have led, routes that continue to exert great influence on my life. I count Rotarians among some of the most creative, courageous, inspiring, and generous people I have ever met. I am proud to be a Rotarian.

The pictures and clippings that follow are from my scrapbook of memorabilia. Perhaps you will recognize some of the subjects.

All profits from the sale of this book will go to the Rotary Foundation.

Memories

Rotary women at One Drop event
Linda Bertuzzi, Sylvia, Raghada Khoury, Teresa Petroff

Some past district governors from District 5300
Garbis der Yeghian; Miles Petroff and spouse, Teresa; Sylvia;
Gene Hernandez; Christine Montan; and Roger Schulte

RI president during my year as governor, Sakuji Tanaka

Celebrating Tijuana's eightieth anniversary
in Rotary with exchange students

The staff of Piyali Learning Center, India
My DG project

Wearing the NIDS jacket and standing in front of Deepa's car

NIDS trip in Delhi

Two strong supporters, PRIPs Keller and Dochterman

NIDS with Gene Hernandez and Anil Garg

First woman at PETS, 1987, with DGE Tim Siu and
PDG Pablo Campos Lynch from Mexico City